HASHIMOTO'S COOKBOOK

MEGA BUNDLE – 2 Manuscripts in 1 – 80+ Hashimoto's - friendly recipes to enjoy diet and live a healthy life

TABLE OF CONTENTS

2

Introduction

Hashimoto's recipes for personal enjoyment but also for family enjoyment. You will love them for sure for how easy it is to prepare them.

BREAKFAST

PRUNES PANCAKES

Serves: **4**

Prep Time: **10** Minutes

Cook Time: **30** Minutes

Total Time: **40** Minutes

INGREDIENTS

- 1 cup whole wheat flour
- ¼ tsp baking soda
- ¼ tsp baking powder
- 2 eggs
- 1 cup milk
- ½ cup prunes

DIRECTIONS

1. In a bowl combine all ingredients together and mix well
2. In a skillet heat olive oil
3. Pour ¼ of the batter and cook each pancake for 1-2 minutes per side
4. When ready remove from heat and serve

Serves: *8-12*

Prep Time: *10*   Minutes

Cook Time: *20*   Minutes

Total Time: *30*   Minutes

INGREDIENTS

- 2 eggs
- 1 tablespoon olive oil
- 1 cup milk
- 2 cups whole wheat flour
- 1 tsp baking soda
- ¼ tsp baking soda
- 1 cup prunes
- 1 tsp cinnamon
- ¼ cup molasses

DIRECTIONS

1. In a bowl combine all wet ingredients
2. In another bowl combine all dry ingredients
3. Combine wet and dry ingredients together
4. Pour mixture into 8-12 prepared muffin cups, fill 2/3 of the cups
5. Bake for 18-20 minutes at 375 F

PLANTAIN MUFFINS

Serves:	*8-12*
Prep Time:	*10* Minutes
Cook Time:	*20* Minutes
Total Time:	*30* Minutes

INGREDIENTS

- 2 eggs
- 1 tablespoon olive oil
- 1 cup milk
- 2 cups whole wheat flour
- 1 tsp baking soda
- ¼ tsp baking soda
- 1 tsp cinnamon
- 1 cup plantain

DIRECTIONS

1. In a bowl combine all wet ingredients
2. In another bowl combine all dry ingredients
3. Combine wet and dry ingredients together
4. Pour mixture into 8-12 prepared muffin cups, fill 2/3 of the cups
5. Bake for 18-20 minutes at 375 F
6. When ready remove from the oven and serve

BLUEBERRY MUFFINS

Serves: **_8-12_**

Prep Time: **_10_**   Minutes

Cook Time: **_20_**   Minutes

Total Time: **_30_**   Minutes

INGREDIENTS

- 2 eggs
- 1 tablespoon olive oil
- 1 cup milk
- 2 cups whole wheat flour
- 1 tsp baking soda
- ¼ tsp baking soda
- 1 tsp cinnamon
- 1 cup blueberries

DIRECTIONS

1. In a bowl combine all wet ingredients
2. In another bowl combine all dry ingredients
3. Combine wet and dry ingredients together
4. Fold in blueberries and mix well
5. Pour mixture into 8-12 prepared muffin cups, fill 2/3 of the cups
6. Bake for 18-20 minutes at 375 F

PUMPKIN MUFFINS

Serves:	*8-12*
Prep Time:	*10* Minutes
Cook Time:	*20* Minutes
Total Time:	*30* Minutes

INGREDIENTS

- 2 eggs
- 1 tablespoon olive oil
- 1 cup milk
- 2 cups whole wheat flour
- 1 tsp baking soda
- ¼ tsp baking soda
- 1 tsp cinnamon
- 1 cup pumpkin puree

DIRECTIONS

1. In a bowl combine all wet ingredients
2. In another bowl combine all dry ingredients
3. Combine wet and dry ingredients together
4. Pour mixture into 8-12 prepared muffin cups, fill 2/3 of the cups
5. Bake for 18-20 minutes at 375 F
6. When ready remove from the oven and serve

CHOCOLATE MUFFINS

Serves: *8-12*
Prep Time: *10*   Minutes

Cook Time: *20*   Minutes

Total Time: *30*   Minutes

INGREDIENTS

- 2 eggs
- 1 tablespoon olive oil
- 1 cup milk
- 2 cups whole wheat flour
- 1 tsp baking soda
- ¼ tsp baking soda
- 1 tsp cinnamon
- 1 cup chocolate chips

DIRECTIONS

1. In a bowl combine all wet ingredients
2. In another bowl combine all dry ingredients
3. Combine wet and dry ingredients together
4. Fold in chocolate chips and mix well
5. Pour mixture into 8-12 prepared muffin cups, fill 2/3 of the cups
6. Bake for 18-20 minutes at 375 F

GOOSEBERRY MUFFINS

Serves: *8-12*
Prep Time: *10*   Minutes

Cook Time: *20*   Minutes

Total Time: *30*   Minutes

INGREDIENTS

- 2 eggs
- 1 tablespoon olive oil
- 1 cup milk
- 2 cups whole wheat flour
- 1 tsp baking soda
- ¼ tsp baking soda
- 1 tsp gooseberries

DIRECTIONS

1. In a bowl combine all wet ingredients
2. In another bowl combine all dry ingredients
3. Combine wet and dry ingredients together
4. Pour mixture into 8-12 prepared muffin cups, fill 2/3 of the cups
5. Bake for 18-20 minutes at 375 F
6. When ready remove from the oven and serve

GOAT CHEESE OMELETTE

Serves: **1**

Prep Time: **5** Minutes

Cook Time: **10** Minutes

Total Time: **15** Minutes

INGREDIENTS

- 2 eggs
- ¼ tsp salt
- ¼ tsp black pepper
- 1 tablespoon olive oil
- ¼ cup goat cheese
- ¼ tsp basil

DIRECTIONS

1. In a bowl combine all ingredients together and mix well
2. In a skillet heat olive oil and pour the egg mixture
3. Cook for 1-2 minutes per side
4. When ready remove omelette from the skillet and serve

ZUCCHINI OMELETTE

Serves: **1**

Prep Time: **5** Minutes

Cook Time: **10** Minutes

Total Time: **15** Minutes

INGREDIENTS

- 2 eggs
- ¼ tsp salt
- ¼ tsp black pepper
- 1 tablespoon olive oil
- ¼ cup cheese
- ¼ tsp basil
- 1 cup zucchini

DIRECTIONS

1. In a bowl combine all ingredients together and mix well
2. In a skillet heat olive oil and pour the egg mixture
3. Cook for 1-2 minutes per side
4. When ready remove omelette from the skillet and serve

ENCHILADA OMELETTE

Serves: *1*

Prep Time: 5   Minutes

Cook Time: *10*   Minutes

Total Time: *15*   Minutes

INGREDIENTS

- 2 eggs
- ¼ tsp salt
- ¼ tsp black pepper
- 1 tablespoon olive oil
- ¼ cup cheese
- ¼ tsp basil
- 1 cup enchilada

DIRECTIONS

1. In a bowl combine all ingredients together and mix well
2. In a skillet heat olive oil and pour the egg mixture
3. Cook for 1-2 minutes per side
4. When ready remove omelette from the skillet and serve

RED ONION OMELETTE

Serves: *1*

Prep Time: 5 Minutes

Cook Time: *10* Minutes

Total Time: *15* Minutes

INGREDIENTS

- 2 eggs
- ¼ tsp salt
- ¼ tsp black pepper
- 1 tablespoon olive oil
- ¼ cup cheese
- ¼ tsp basil
- 1 cup red onion

DIRECTIONS

1. In a bowl combine all ingredients together and mix well
2. In a skillet heat olive oil and pour the egg mixture
3. Cook for 1-2 minutes per side
4. When ready remove omelette from the skillet and serve

TOMATO OMELETTE

Serves: *1*

Prep Time: *5*   Minutes

Cook Time: *10*   Minutes

Total Time: *15*   Minutes

INGREDIENTS

- 2 eggs
- ¼ tsp salt
- ¼ tsp black pepper
- 1 tablespoon olive oil
- ¼ cup cheese
- ¼ tsp basil
- 1 cup tomatoes

DIRECTIONS

1. In a bowl combine all ingredients together and mix well
2. In a skillet heat olive oil and pour the egg mixture
3. Cook for 1-2 minutes per side
4. When ready remove omelette from the skillet and serve

BLUEBERRIES GRANOLA

Serves: *2*

Prep Time: *10*   Minutes

Cook Time: *40*   Minutes

Total Time: *50*   Minutes

INGREDIENTS

- 1 cup blueberries
- 2 cup porridge oats
- 2 oz. coconut flakes
- 2 oz. brown sugar
- 2 tablespoons honey
- 1/2 cup raisins
- 1 cup chocolate chips

DIRECTIONS

1. In a bowl combine all ingredients together and mix well
2. Spread mixture on a baking sheet
3. Bake at 275 F for 30-40 minutes
4. When ready remove from the oven, cut into bars and serve

CARROT CAKE GRANOLA

Serves: **4-6**

Prep Time: **10** Minutes

Cook Time: **40** Minutes

Total Time: **50** Minutes

INGREDIENTS

- 1 cup oats
- 1 tsp mixed spice
- ¼ lb. walnuts
- 2 carrots
- 2 oz. coconut oil
- 2 oz. honey

DIRECTIONS

1. In a bowl combine all ingredients together and mix well
2. Place the mixture into a baking dish
3. Bake at 350 F for 30-40 minutes
4. When ready remove from the oven and serve

Serves: **6-8**

Prep Time: **10** Minutes

Cook Time: **40** Minutes

Total Time: **50** Minutes

INGREDIENTS

- ¼ lb. butter
- 2 cups oats
- ¼ lb. sunflower seeds
- 2 oz. sesame seeds
- 2 oz. walnuts
- 2 tablespoons honey
- 1 tsp cinnamon
- 1 cup cherries
- 1 cup blueberries

DIRECTIONS

1. In a bowl combine all ingredients together and mix well
2. Place the mixture into a baking dish
3. Bake at 350 F for 30-40 minutes
4. When ready remove from the oven cut into bars and serve

ORANGE GRANOLA

Serves: **6-8**

Prep Time: **10**   Minutes

Cook Time: **35**   Minutes

Total Time: **45**   Minutes

INGREDIENTS

- 1 lb. oats
- Juice from 1 orange
- 1 tsp cinnamon
- 2 oz. almonds
- 2 oz. sunflower seeds

DIRECTIONS

1. Place all ingredients, except orange juice, in a blender and blend until smooth
2. In a saucepan boil the orange juice and mix with the mixture and cook until the liquid has evaporated
3. Spread the mixture on a baking sheet
4. Bake at 350 F for 15-20 minutes
5. When ready remove from the oven cut into bars and serve

FRENCH TOAST

Serves: *4*
Prep Time: *10*   Minutes

Cook Time: *20*   Minutes

Total Time: *30*   Minutes

INGREDIENTS

- 1 tablespoon olive oil
- 4 eggs
- 100 ml double cream
- ¼ tsp cinnamon
- ¼ tsp nutmeg
- ¼ tsp peanut butter
- 4 bread slices

DIRECTIONS

1. In a bowl combine all ingredients together and mix well
2. Place the bread into the dipping and let the bread soak for 3-4 minutes
3. In a skillet heat olive oil and fry the bread for 2-3 minutes per side
4. When ready remove from the skillet and serve

BEANS OMELETTE

Serves: *1*

Prep Time: *5*   Minutes

Cook Time: *10*   Minutes

Total Time: *15*   Minutes

INGREDIENTS

- 2 eggs
- ¼ tsp salt
- ¼ tsp black pepper
- 1 tablespoon olive oil
- ¼ cup cheese
- ¼ tsp basil
- 1 cup beans

DIRECTIONS

1. In a bowl combine all ingredients together and mix well
2. In a skillet heat olive oil and pour the egg mixture
3. Cook for 1-2 minutes per side
4. When ready remove omelette from the skillet and serve

BREAKFAST GRANOLA

Serves: 2

Prep Time: 5 Minutes

Cook Time: 30 Minutes

Total Time: 35 Minutes

INGREDIENTS

- 1 tsp vanilla extract
- 1 tablespoon honey
- 1 lb. rolled oats
- 2 tablespoons sesame seeds
- ¼ lb. almonds
- ¼ lb. berries

DIRECTIONS

1. Preheat the oven to 325 F
2. Spread the granola onto a baking sheet
3. Bake for 12-15 minutes, remove and mix everything
4. Bake for another 12-15 minutes or until slightly brown
5. When ready remove from the oven and serve

BLUEBERRY PANCAKES

Serves: **4**

Prep Time: **10** Minutes

Cook Time: **20** Minutes

Total Time: **30** Minutes

INGREDIENTS

- 1 cup whole wheat flour
- ¼ tsp baking soda
- ¼ tsp baking powder
- 1 cup blueberries
- 1 cup milk

DIRECTIONS

1. In a bowl combine all ingredients together and mix well
2. In a skillet heat olive oil
3. Pour ¼ of the batter and cook each pancake for 1-2 minutes per side
4. When ready remove from heat and serve

CURRANTS PANCAKES

Serves: **4**

Prep Time: **10** Minutes

Cook Time: **30** Minutes

Total Time: **40** Minutes

INGREDIENTS

- 1 cup whole wheat flour
- ¼ tsp baking soda
- ¼ tsp baking powder
- 1 cup currants
- 1 cup milk

DIRECTIONS

1. In a bowl combine all ingredients together and mix well
2. In a skillet heat olive oil
3. Pour ¼ of the batter and cook each pancake for 1-2 minutes per side
4. When ready remove from heat and serve

COCONUT PANCAKES

Serves: *4*

Prep Time: *10*   Minutes

Cook Time: *20*   Minutes

Total Time: *30*   Minutes

INGREDIENTS

- 1 cup whole wheat flour
- ¼ tsp baking soda
- ¼ tsp baking powder
- ¼ cup coconut flakes
- 1 cup milk

DIRECTIONS

1. In a bowl combine all ingredients together and mix well
2. In a skillet heat olive oil
3. Pour ¼ of the batter and cook each pancake for 1-2 minutes per side
4. When ready remove from heat and serve

Serves: **4**

Prep Time: **10**   Minutes

Cook Time: **20**   Minutes

Total Time: **30**   Minutes

INGREDIENTS

- 1 cup whole wheat flour
- ¼ tsp baking soda
- ¼ tsp baking powder
- 1 cup coconut flakes
- 1 cup milk

DIRECTIONS

1. In a bowl combine all ingredients together and mix well
2. In a skillet heat olive oil
3. Pour ¼ of the batter and cook each pancake for 1-2 minutes per side
4. When ready remove from heat and serve

PANCAKES

Serves: *4*
Prep Time: *10*   Minutes

Cook Time: *30*   Minutes

Total Time: *40*   Minutes

INGREDIENTS

- 1 cup whole wheat flour
- ¼ tsp baking soda
- ¼ tsp baking powder
- 1 cup milk

DIRECTIONS

1. In a bowl combine all ingredients together and mix well
2. In a skillet heat olive oil
3. Pour ¼ of the batter and cook each pancake for 1-2 minutes per side
4. When ready remove from heat and serve

RAISIN BREAKFAST MIX

Serves: **1**

Prep Time: **5** Minutes

Cook Time: **5** Minutes

Total Time: **10** Minutes

INGREDIENTS

- ½ cup dried raisins
- ½ cup dried pecans
- ¼ cup almonds
- 1 cup coconut milk
- 1 tsp cinnamon

DIRECTIONS

1. In a bowl combine all ingredients together
2. Serve with milk

Serves: **2**

Prep Time: **5**   Minutes

Cook Time: **15**   Minutes

Total Time: **20**   Minutes

INGREDIENTS

- ¼ cup egg substitute
- 1 muffin
- 1 turkey sausage patty
- 1 tablespoon cheddar cheese

DIRECTIONS

1. In a skillet pour egg and cook on low heat
2. Place turkey sausage patty in a pan and cook for 4-5 minutes per side
3. On a toasted muffin place the cooked egg, top with a sausage patty and cheddar cheese
4. Serve when ready

STRAWBERRY MUFFINS

Serves: **8-12**

Prep Time: **10** Minutes

Cook Time: **20** Minutes

Total Time: **30** Minutes

INGREDIENTS

- 2 eggs
- 1 tablespoon olive oil
- 1 cup milk
- 2 cups whole wheat flour
- 1 tsp baking soda
- ¼ tsp baking soda
- 1 tsp cinnamon
- 1 cup strawberries

DIRECTIONS

1. In a bowl combine all wet ingredients
2. In another bowl combine all dry ingredients
3. Combine wet and dry ingredients together
4. Pour mixture into 8-12 prepared muffin cups, fill 2/3 of the cups
5. Bake for 18-20 minutes at 375 F
6. When ready remove from the oven and serve

DESSERTS

BREAKFAST COOKIES

Serves: *8-12*

Prep Time: 5   Minutes

Cook Time: *15*   Minutes

Total Time: *20*   Minutes

INGREDIENTS

- 1 cup rolled oats
- ¼ cup applesauce
- ½ tsp vanilla extract
- 3 tablespoons chocolate chips
- 2 tablespoons dried fruits
- 1 tsp cinnamon

DIRECTIONS

1. Preheat the oven to 325 F
2. In a bowl combine all ingredients together and mix well
3. Scoop cookies using an ice cream scoop
4. Place cookies onto a prepared baking sheet
5. Place in the oven for 12-15 minutes or until the cookies are done
6. When ready remove from the oven and serve

BLUEBERRY PIE

Serves: *8-12*

Prep Time: *15*   Minutes

Cook Time: *35*   Minutes

Total Time: *50*   Minutes

INGREDIENTS

- pastry sheets
- ¼ tsp lavender
- 1 cup brown sugar
- 4-5 cups blueberries
- 1 tablespoon lemon juice
- 1 cup almonds
- 2 tablespoons butter

DIRECTIONS

1. Line a pie plate or pie form with pastry and cover the edges of the plate depending on your preference
2. In a bowl combine all pie ingredients together and mix well
3. Pour the mixture over the pastry
4. Bake at 400-425 F for 25-30 minutes or until golden brown
5. When ready remove from the oven and let it rest for 15 minutes

Serves:	*8-12*	
Prep Time:	*15*	Minutes
Cook Time:	*35*	Minutes
Total Time:	*50*	Minutes

INGREDIENTS

- pastry sheets
- 1 cup buttermilk
- 1 can pumpkin
- 1 cup sugar
- 1 tsp cinnamon
- 1 tsp vanilla extract
- 2 eggs

DIRECTIONS

1. Line a pie plate or pie form with pastry and cover the edges of the plate depending on your preference
2. In a bowl combine all pie ingredients together and mix well
3. Pour the mixture over the pastry
4. Bake at 400-425 F for 25-30 minutes or until golden brown
5. When ready remove from the oven and let it rest for 15 minutes

RICOTTA ICE-CREAM

Serves: *6-8*

Prep Time: *15*   Minutes

Cook Time: *15*   Minutes

Total Time: *30*   Minutes

INGREDIENTS

- 1 cup almonds
- 1-pint vanilla ice cream
- 2 cups ricotta cheese
- 1 cup honey

DIRECTIONS

1. In a saucepan whisk together all ingredients
2. Mix until bubbly
3. Strain into a bowl and cool
4. Whisk in favorite fruits and mix well
5. Cover and refrigerate for 2-3 hours
6. Pour mixture in the ice-cream maker and follow manufacturer instructions
7. Serve when ready

SAFFRON ICE-CREAM

Serves: *6-8*

Prep Time: *15*   Minutes
Cook Time: *15*   Minutes
Total Time: *30*   Minutes

INGREDIENTS

- 4 egg yolks
- 1 cup heavy cream
- 1 cup milk
- ½ cup brown sugar
- 1 tsp saffron
- 1 tsp vanilla extract

DIRECTIONS

1. In a saucepan whisk together all ingredients
2. Mix until bubbly
3. Strain into a bowl and cool
4. Whisk in favorite fruits and mix well
5. Cover and refrigerate for 2-3 hours
6. Pour mixture in the ice-cream maker and follow manufacturer instructions
7. Serve when ready

SMOOTHIES AND DRINKS

FIG SMOOTHIE

Serves: **1**

Prep Time: **5**   Minutes

Cook Time: **5**   Minutes

Total Time: **10**   Minutes

INGREDIENTS

- 1 cup ice
- 1 cup vanilla yogurt
- 1 cup coconut milk
- 1 tsp honey
- 4 figs

DIRECTIONS

1. In a blender place all ingredients and blend until smooth
2. Pour smoothie in a glass and serve

POMEGRANATE SMOOTHIE

Serves: **1**

Prep Time: 5   Minutes

Cook Time: 5   Minutes

Total Time: **10**   Minutes

INGREDIENTS

- 2 cups blueberries
- 1 cup pomegranate
- 1 tablespoon honey
- 1 cup Greek yogurt

DIRECTIONS

1. In a blender place all ingredients and blend until smooth
2. Pour smoothie in a glass and serve

GINGER-KALE SMOOTHIE

Serves: *1*

Prep Time: *5* Minutes

Cook Time: *5* Minutes

Total Time: *10* Minutes

INGREDIENTS

- 1 cup kale
- 1 banana
- 1 cup almond milk
- 1 cup vanilla yogurt
- 1 tsp chia seeds
- ¼ tsp ginger

DIRECTIONS

1. In a blender place all ingredients and blend until smooth
2. Pour smoothie in a glass and serve

BERRY YOGHURT SMOOTHIE

Serves: *1*

Prep Time: 5   Minutes

Cook Time: 5   Minutes

Total Time: *10*   Minutes

INGREDIENTS

- 6 oz. berries
- 2 bananas
- 4 oz. vanilla yoghurt
- 1 cup milk
- 1 tablespoon honey

DIRECTIONS

1. In a blender place all ingredients and blend until smooth
2. Pour smoothie in a glass and serve

COCONUT SMOOTHIE

Serves: *1*

Prep Time: *5*   Minutes

Cook Time: *5*   Minutes

Total Time: *10*   Minutes

INGREDIENTS

- 2 mangoes
- 2 bananas
- 1 cup coconut water
- 1 cup ice
- 1 tablespoon honey
- 1 cup Greek Yoghurt
- 1 cup strawberries

DIRECTIONS

1. In a blender place all ingredients and blend until smooth
2. Pour smoothie in a glass and serve

RASPBERRY-VANILLA SMOOTHIE

Serves: **1**

Prep Time: **5**   Minutes

Cook Time: **5**   Minutes

Total Time: **10**   Minutes

INGREDIENTS

- ¼ cup sugar
- ¼ cup water
- 1 cup Greek yoghurt
- 1 cup raspberries
- 1 tsp vanilla extract
- 1 cup ice

DIRECTIONS

1. In a blender place all ingredients and blend until smooth
2. Pour smoothie in a glass and serve

CHERRY SMOOTHIE

Serves: *1*

Prep Time: *5*   Minutes

Cook Time: *5*   Minutes

Total Time: *10*   Minutes

INGREDIENTS

- 1 can cherries
- 2 tablespoons peanut butter
- 1 tablespoon honey
- 1 cup Greek Yoghurt
- 1 cup coconut milk

DIRECTIONS

1. In a blender place all ingredients and blend until smooth
2. Pour smoothie in a glass and serve

CHOCOLATE SMOOTHIE

Serves: *1*

Prep Time: *5*   Minutes

Cook Time: *5*   Minutes

Total Time: *10* Minutes

INGREDIENTS

- 2 bananas
- 1 cup Greek Yoghurt
- 1 tablespoon honey
- 1 tablespoon cocoa powder
- ½ cup chocolate chips
- ¼ cup almond milk

DIRECTIONS

1. In a blender place all ingredients and blend until smooth
2. Pour smoothie in a glass and serve

TOFU SMOOTHIE

Serves: *1*

Prep Time: *5*   Minutes

Cook Time: *5*   Minutes

Total Time: *10*   Minutes

INGREDIENTS

- 1 cup blueberries
- ¼ cup tofu
- ¼ cup pomegranate juice
- 1 cup ice
- ½ cup agave nectar

DIRECTIONS

1. In a blender place all ingredients and blend until smooth
2. Pour smoothie in a glass and serve

Serves: *1*
Prep Time: 5   Minutes

Cook Time: 5   Minutes

Total Time: *10*   Minutes

INGREDIENTS

- 1 orange
- ½ cup orange juice
- ½ banana
- 1 tsp vanilla essence

DIRECTIONS

1. In a blender place all ingredients and blend until smooth
2. Pour smoothie in a glass and serve

Serves: *1*

Prep Time: *5* Minutes

Cook Time: *5* Minutes

Total Time: *10* Minutes

INGREDIENTS

- ¼ cup raisins
- 2 Medjool dates
- 1 cup berries
- 1 cup almond milk
- 1 tsp chia seeds

DIRECTIONS

1. In a blender place all ingredients and blend until smooth
2. Pour smoothie in a glass and serve

SECOND COOKBOOK

SOUP RECIPES

ZUCCHINI SOUP

Serves: **4**

Prep Time: **10** Minutes

Cook Time: **20** Minutes

Total Time: **30** Minutes

INGREDIENTS

- 1 tablespoon olive oil
- 1 lb. zucchini
- ¼ red onion
- ½ cup all-purpose flour
- ¼ tsp salt
- ¼ tsp pepper
- 1 can vegetable broth
- 1 cup heavy cream

DIRECTIONS

1. In a saucepan heat olive oil and sauté zucchini until tender
2. Add remaining ingredients to the saucepan and bring to a boil
3. When all the vegetables are tender transfer to a blender and blend until smooth
4. Pour soup into bowls, garnish with parsley and serve

BROCCOLI SOUP

Serves: *2*

Prep Time: *10*   Minutes

Cook Time: *10*   Minutes

Total Time: *20*   Minutes

INGREDIENTS

- 1 onion
- 2 cloves garlic
- 1 tbs butter
- 2 cup broccoli
- 1 potato
- 3 cup chicken broth
- 1 cup cheddar cheese
- 1/3 cup buttermilk
- Salt
- Pepper

DIRECTIONS

1. Cook the onion and garlic in melted butter for 5 minutes
2. Add the diced potato, broccoli florets and chicken broth
3. Bring to a boil, then reduce the heat and simmer for at least 5 minutes
4. Allow to cool, then pulse until smooth using a blender

5. Return to the saucepan and add the buttermilk and ¼ cup cheese
6. Cook for about 3 minutes
7. Season with salt and pepper
8. Serve topped with the remaining cheese

Serves: **6**

Prep Time: **40**   Minutes

Cook Time: **80**   Minutes

Total Time: **120**   Minutes

INGREDIENTS

Broth:
- 15 peppercorns
- 2 onions
- 2 carrots
- 1 rib celery
- 3 sprigs thyme
- 5 cloves garlic
- 3 bay leaves
- 8 chicken thighs

Soup:
- 2 chicken bouillon cubes
- 1 tsp salt
- 5 oz egg noodles
- 1/3 cup parsley
- 2 ribs celery
- 2 carrots

DIRECTIONS

1. Place the broth ingredients in a pot with 12 cups of water
2. Bring to a boil, then reduce the heat and simmer for about 20 minutes
3. Remove the chicken and shred meat from bones
4. Return the bones to the pot and continue to simmer for another 60 minutes
5. Strain the broth and discard the bones and other solids
6. Skim broth and bring to a boil
7. Add the soup ingredients except for the parsley
8. Stir in the noodles and cook for at least 5 minutes
9. Stir in the chicken meat and parsley and cook 1 more minute
10. Serve immediately

TORTILLA SOUP

Serves: *6*

Prep Time: *10*   Minutes

Cook Time: *10*   Minutes

Total Time: *20*   Minutes

INGREDIENTS

- 1/3 cup rice
- 15 oz salsa
- 1 can black beans
- 30 oz chicken broth
- 1 cup corn
- Chicken

DIRECTIONS

1. Place the broth and the salsa in a pot and bring to a boil
2. Add rice, beans and cooked chicken
3. Simmer covered for about 10 minutes
4. Stir in the corn
5. Serve topped with cheese

ASPARAGUS SOUP

Serves: *4*

Prep Time: *15*   Minutes

Cook Time: *35*   Minutes

Total Time: *50*   Minutes

INGREDIENTS

- 2 tbs oil
- 1/3 tsp salt
- 1 cup bread cubes
- 1 cup potato
- 2 tsp horseradish
- 3 cups chicken broth
- 1 lb asparagus
- Scallions
- 1 shallot

DIRECTIONS

1. Cook the shallot until soft for 2 minutes
2. Add the asparagus, potato, broth, horseradish and salt and bring to a boil
3. Reduce the heat and simmer for about 15 minutes
4. Pulse using a blender
5. Cook the bread cubes in hot oil until crispy, serve with croutons

LENTIL SOUP

Serves: *9*
Prep Time: *10* Minutes

Cook Time: *50* Minutes

Total Time: *60* Minutes

INGREDIENTS

- 2 tbs oil
- 1 stalk celery
- 1 red bell pepper
- 2 cans chicken broth
- 1 onion
- 1 cup carrots
- 2 garlic cloves
- 2 tsp cumin
- 1 tsp coriander
- 1 can tomatoes
- 2 sweet potatoes
- 3 tsp thyme leaves
- 2 cups red lentils

DIRECTIONS

1. Cook the onion, celery, carrots and red pepper in hot oil for 3 minutes

2. Add garlic, thyme, cumin and coriander and cook for 10 more minutes
3. Add the broth, sweet potatoes, lentils and tomatoes
4. Bring to a boil, then reduce the heat and simmer for at least 30 minutes
5. Pulse using a blender
6. Serve immediately

Serves: **4**

Prep Time: **10** Minutes

Cook Time: **15** Minutes

Total Time: **25** Minutes

INGREDIENTS

- 1 cup broccoli florets
- 1 cup red capsicum
- 1 tsp oil
- 1 tablespoon garlic
- ¼ cup onions
- pinch of salt
- 1 tsp pepper powder

DIRECTIONS

1. In a pan sauté onions and garlic for 2-3 minutes
2. Add salt, red capsicum, broccoli, 1 cup water, and mix well
3. Cover with a lid cook for 5-6 minutes
4. When ready remove from heat and blend using a mixer
5. Transfer the mixture back to the pan, add ¼ cup water, pepper powder and cook for another 2-3 minutes
6. When ready remove from heat and serve

CANTALOUPE SOUP

Serves: **4**

Prep Time: **10**   Minutes

Cook Time: **15**   Minutes

Total Time: **25**   Minutes

INGREDIENTS

- 2 cantaloupes
- 1 tsp ginger
- ½ tsp nutmeg
- ½ cup fat-free sour cream

DIRECTIONS

1. Remove seeds from cantaloupes and refrigerate
2. Pour melon into a blender with spices, sour cream and blend until smooth
3. Refrigerate for another hour and pour soup into the bowl
4. Garnish with nutmeg, ginger and serve

GREEN PESTO PASTA

Serves: **2**

Prep Time: **5**   Minutes

Cook Time: **15** Minutes

Total Time: **20** Minutes

INGREDIENTS

- 4 oz. spaghetti
- 2 cups basil leaves
- 2 garlic cloves
- ¼ cup olive oil
- 2 tablespoons parmesan cheese
- ½ tsp black pepper

DIRECTIONS

1. Bring water to a boil and add pasta
2. In a blend add parmesan cheese, basil leaves, garlic and blend
3. Add olive oil, pepper and blend again
4. Pour pesto onto pasta and serve when ready

Serves: **4**

Prep Time: **5**   Minutes

Cook Time: **20**   Minutes

Total Time: **25**   Minutes

INGREDIENTS

- 1 cup buckwheat
- 1 tablespoon olive oil
- 1 tsp mustard seeds
- ½ tsp asafetida
- 1 tsp green chilies
- 1 tablespoon coriander
- 1 tablespoon urad dal

DIRECTIONS

1. In a bowl combine urad dal and buckwheat, using a mixer blend until smooth
2. In a pan add mustard seeds, asafetida, chilies, salt, coriander, water, and mix well
3. Pour 1/3 cup batter in a circular manner and cook until golden brown
4. When ready remove and serve

Serves: **3**

Prep Time: **10** Minutes

Cook Time: **30** Minutes

Total Time: **40** Minutes

INGREDIENTS

- ½ cup zucchini
- ¼ cup bajra
- 1 tsp olive oil
- 1 tsp cumin seeds
- ¼ cup red capsicum
- ¼ cup green capsicum
- ¼ cup almond milk
- ¼ tsp chili paste
- ¼ cup coriander

DIRECTIONS

1. Soak the bajra in water overnight
2. In a pressure cooker combine water, bajra and mix well
3. Allow the steam to go away before opening the lid
4. In a pan add cumin seeds, asafetida and sauté for 1-2 minutes
5. Add capsicum, zucchini, salt and sauté for another 3-4 minutes

6. Add milk, coriander, chili paste and cook for another 2-3 minutes
7. When ready remove from heat and serve

QUINOA MUTHIA

Serves: *5*
Prep Time: *10*   Minutes

Cook Time: *40*   Minutes

Total Time: *50*   Minutes

INGREDIENTS

- ½ cup quinoa flour
- 1 cup besan
- ¼ cup semolina
- 1 cup bottle gourd
- 6 tsp oil
- 2 tsp chilli paste
- 1 pinch baking soda
- ¼ tsp asafetida
- ¼ tsp turmeric powder
- 1 tsp lemon juice
- 1 tsp mustard seeds
- 1 tsp sesame seeds
- 3 curry leaves
- 1 tablespoon coriander

DIRECTIONS

1. In a bowl combine semolina, besan, quinoa flour, 1 tsp oil, chili paste, gourd, asafetida, turmeric powder, lemon juice, and salt

2. Divide mixture into 4-5 portions and shape them into patties

3. Steam in a steamer for 10-15 minutes

4. When ready, remove from the steamer

5. In a pan add remaining oil, sesame seeds, curry leaves, asafetida and sauté for 1 minute

6. Add muthia, sauté for 2-3 minutes and serve with coriander

LIME GRILLED CORN

Serves: *3*
Prep Time: *5*   Minutes
Cook Time: *15*   Minutes
Total Time: *20*   Minutes

INGREDIENTS

- 3 ears of corn
- 2 tablespoons mayonnaise
- 2 tablespoons squeezed lime juice
- ½ tsp chili powder
- 1 pinch of salt

DIRECTIONS

1. Place corn onto the grill and cook for 5-6 minutes or until the kernels being to brown
2. Turn every few minutes until all sides are slightly charred
3. In a bowl mix the rest of ingredients
4. Spread a light coating of the mixture onto each corn and serve

Serves: *5*

Prep Time: *10* Minutes

Cook Time: *15* Minutes

Total Time: *25* Minutes

INGREDIENTS

- 2 cups capsicum cubes
- ¼ cup paneer
- 1 tsp oil
- ¼ cup onion cubes
- ¼ tsp ginger paste
- 1 tsp garlic paste
- 1 tsp dried fenugreek leaves
- 1 cup tomato pulp
- ¼ tsp turmeric powder
- ¼ tsp chili powder
- 1 tsp garam masala
- pinch of salt

DIRECTIONS

1. In a pan sauté onion
2. Add garlic paste, fenugreek leaves, ginger paste and sauté for 1 minute

3. Add capsicum, turmeric powder, tomato pulp, chili powder, garam masala and mix well

4. Cook for 5-6 minutes, add salt, paneer and mix well

5. Cook for another 2-3 minutes, when ready remove from heat and serve

AVOCADO DIP

Serves: **4**

Prep Time: 5   Minutes

Cook Time: 5   Minutes

Total Time: **10**   Minutes

INGREDIENTS

- 1 cup mashed avocado
- 1 tsp lemon juice
- 1 tablespoon tomatoes
- ¼ tsp green chilies
- pinch of salt

DIRECTIONS

1. In a bowl combine all ingredients together and mix well
2. When ready serve with corn chips

Serves: *28*

Prep Time: *5*   Minutes

Cook Time: *20*   Minutes

Total Time: *25*   Minutes

INGREDIENTS

- ½ cup jowar
- ½ cup onions
- 1 tsp sesame seeds
- pinch of salt
- ¼ tsp oil

DIRECTIONS

1. In a bowl combine all ingredients together
2. Divide dough into 22-28 portions
3. Press each portion of dough between your hands until it looks like a thin circle
4. Grease a baking tray with oil
5. Bake for 18-20 minutes at 350 F
6. When ready remove and serve

KALE CHIPS

Serves: **6**

Prep Time: **10** Minutes

Cook Time: **25** Minutes

Total Time: **35** Minutes

INGREDIENTS

- 1 bunch of kale
- 1 tablespoon olive oil
- 1 tsp salt

DIRECTIONS

1. Preheat the oven to 325 F
2. Chop the kale into chip size pieces
3. Put pieces into a bowl tops with olive oil and salt
4. Spread the leaves in a single layer onto a parchment paper
5. Bake for 20-25 minutes
6. When ready, remove and serve

CRANBERRY SALAD

Serves: **2**

Prep Time: **5** Minutes

Cook Time: **5** Minutes

Total Time: **10** Minutes

INGREDIENTS

- 1 can unsweetened pineapple
- 1 package cherry gelatin
- 1 tablespoon lemon juice
- ½ cup artificial sweetener
- 1 cup cranberries
- 1 orange
- 1 cup celery
- ½ cup pecans

DIRECTIONS

1. In a bowl mix all ingredients and mix well
2. Serve with dressing

Serves: *2*
Prep Time: *5*   Minutes

Cook Time: *5*   Minutes

Total Time: *10*   Minutes

INGREDIENTS

- 8 oz. romaine lettuce
- 2 cups radicchio
- ¼ red onion
- 2 ribs celery
- 1 cup tomatoes
- 1 can chickpeas
- 1 cup salad dressing

DIRECTIONS

1. In a bowl mix all ingredients and mix well
2. Serve with dressing

Serves: 2
Prep Time: 5   Minutes

Cook Time: 5   Minutes

Total Time: 10   Minutes

INGREDIENTS

- 2 cans chickpeas
- 2 cups carrots
- 1 cup celery
- ¼ cup green onions
- ¼ cup dill leaves
- ¼ cup olive oil
- 1 cucumber
- 1 cup salad dressing

DIRECTIONS

1. In a bowl mix all ingredients and mix well
2. Serve with dressing

Serves: **2**

Prep Time: **5**   Minutes

Cook Time: **5**   Minutes

Total Time: **10**   Minutes

INGREDIENTS

- 1 cup cooked quinoa
- 1 cup sunflower seeds
- 1 tablespoon olive oil
- 1 head romaine lettuce
- 1 cup carrots
- 1 cup cabbage
- ¼ cup radishes

DIRECTIONS

1. In a bowl mix all ingredients and mix well
2. Serve with dressing

Serves: **2**

Prep Time: **5**   Minutes

Cook Time: **5**   Minutes

Total Time: **10**   Minutes

INGREDIENTS

- 1 bunch coriander leaves
- 1 bunch mint leaves
- ¼ red onion
- 1 bunch parsley
- 1 cup lentils
- 1 tablespoon pumpkin seeds
- 1 tablespoon pine nuts

DIRECTIONS

1. In a bowl mix all ingredients and mix well
2. Serve with dressing

QUINOA SALAD

Serves: **2**

Prep Time: **5**   Minutes

Cook Time: **5**   Minutes

Total Time: **10** Minutes

INGREDIENTS

- 1 cauliflower
- 2 cups cooked quinoa
- 1 can chickpeas
- 1 cup baby spinach
- ¼ cup parsley
- ¼ cup cilantro
- ¼ cup green onion
- ½ cup feta cheese

DIRECTIONS

1. In a bowl mix all ingredients and mix well
2. Serve with dressing

Serves: *2*

Prep Time: *5*   Minutes

Cook Time: *5*   Minutes

Total Time: *10*   Minutes

INGREDIENTS

- 1 head romaine lettuce
- 1 cup tomatoes
- 1 cup cucumber
- 1 cup celery
- ¼ cup olives
- 1 shallot
- 1 cup salad dressing

DIRECTIONS

1. In a bowl mix all ingredients and mix well
2. Serve with dressing

COUSCOUS SALAD

Serves: **2**
Prep Time: **5**   Minutes

Cook Time: **5**   Minutes

Total Time: **10**   Minutes

INGREDIENTS

- 1 cup couscous
- ¼ cup pine nuts
- ¼ cup olive lil
- 1 tablespoon lemon juice
- 1 shallot
- 2 cloves garlic
- 1 tsp salt
- 1 can chickpeas
- 1 cup tomatoes
- ½ cup feta cheese
- 1 zucchini
- 1 tablespoon basil

DIRECTIONS

1. In a bowl mix all ingredients and mix well
2. Serve with dressing

Serves: **2**

Prep Time: **5**   Minutes

Cook Time: **5**   Minutes

Total Time: ***10***   Minutes

INGREDIENTS

- 1 cup cooked FARRO
- 1 bay leaf
- 1 shallot
- ¼ cup olive oil
- 2 cups arugula
- ¼ cup parmesan cheese
- ¼ cup basil
- ¼ cup parsley
- ¼ cup pecans

DIRECTIONS

1. In a bowl mix all ingredients and mix well
2. Serve with dressing

THAI MANGO SALAD

Serves: **2**

Prep Time: **5**   Minutes

Cook Time: **5**   Minutes

Total Time: **10**   Minutes

INGREDIENTS

- 1 head leaf lettuce
- 1 red bell pepper
- 2 mangoes
- ¼ green onion
- ¼ cup peanuts
- ¼ cup cilantro
- 1 cup peanut dressing

DIRECTIONS

1. In a bowl mix all ingredients and mix well
2. Serve with dressing

LENTIL FRITATTA

Serves:	**2**
Prep Time:	**10** Minutes
Cook Time:	**20** Minutes
Total Time:	**30** Minutes

INGREDIENTS

- ½ lb. lentil
- 1 tablespoon olive oil
- ½ red onion
- ¼ tsp salt
- 2 eggs
- 2 oz. cheddar cheese
- 1 garlic clove
- ¼ tsp dill

DIRECTIONS

1. In a bowl whisk eggs with salt and cheese
2. In a frying pan heat olive oil and pour egg mixture
3. Add remaining ingredients and mix well
4. Serve when ready

SPINACH FRITATTA

Serves: *2*

Prep Time: *10*   Minutes

Cook Time: *20*   Minutes

Total Time: *30*   Minutes

INGREDIENTS

- ½ lb. spinach
- 1 tablespoon olive oil
- ½ red onion
- 2 eggs
- ¼ tsp salt
- 2 oz. cheddar cheese
- 1 garlic clove
- ¼ tsp dill

DIRECTIONS

1. In a skillet sauté spinach until tender
2. In a bowl whisk eggs with salt and cheese
3. In a frying pan heat olive oil and pour egg mixture
4. Add remaining ingredients and mix well
5. When ready serve with sautéed spinach

BLACK BEAN FRITATTA

Serves: **2**

Prep Time: **10**   Minutes

Cook Time: **20**   Minutes

Total Time: **30**   Minutes

INGREDIENTS

- 1 cup cooked black beans
- 1 tablespoon olive oil
- ½ red onion
- ¼ tsp salt
- 2 oz. cheddar cheese
- 1 garlic clove
- ¼ tsp dill
- 2 eggs

DIRECTIONS

1. In a bowl whisk eggs with salt and cheese
2. In a frying pan heat olive oil and pour egg mixture
3. Add remaining ingredients and mix well
4. Serve when ready

CHEESE FRITATTA

Serves: *2*

Prep Time: *10*   Minutes

Cook Time: *20*   Minutes

Total Time: *30*   Minutes

INGREDIENTS

- 1 tablespoon olive oil
- ½ red onion
- ¼ tsp salt
- 2 oz. cheddar cheese
- 1 garlic clove
- ¼ tsp dill
- 2 eggs

DIRECTIONS

1. In a bowl combine cheddar cheese and onion
2. In a frying pan heat olive oil and pour egg mixture
3. Add remaining ingredients and mix well
4. Serve when ready

BROCCOLI FRITATTA

Serves: **2**

Prep Time: **10** Minutes

Cook Time: **20** Minutes

Total Time: **30** Minutes

INGREDIENTS

- 1 cup broccoli
- 1 tablespoon olive oil
- ½ red onion
- ¼ tsp salt
- 2 oz. cheddar cheese
- 1 garlic clove
- 2 eggs
- ¼ tsp dill

DIRECTIONS

1. In a skillet sauté broccoli until tender
2. In a bowl whisk eggs with salt and cheese
3. In a frying pan heat olive oil and pour egg mixture
4. Add remaining ingredients and mix well
5. When ready serve with sautéed broccoli

SHAKSHUKA

Serves: **2**

Prep Time: **10** Minutes

Cook Time: **20** Minutes

Total Time: **30** Minutes

INGREDIENTS

- 1 tablespoon olive oil
- 1 red onion
- 1 red chili
- 1 garlic clove
- 2 cans cherry tomatoes
- 2 eggs

DIRECTIONS

1. In a frying pan cook garlic, chili, onions until soft
2. Stir in tomatoes and cook until mixture thickens
3. Crack the eggs over the sauce
4. Cover with a lid and cook for another 7-8 minutes
5. When ready remove from heat and serve

BROCCOLI CASSEROLE

Serves: **4**

Prep Time: **10**   Minutes

Cook Time: **15**   Minutes

Total Time: **25**   Minutes

INGREDIENTS

- 1 onion
- 2 chicken breasts
- 2 tablespoons unsalted butter
- 2 eggs
- 2 cups cooked rice
- 2 cups cheese
- 1 cup parmesan cheese
- 2 cups cooked broccoli

DIRECTIONS

1. Sauté the veggies and set aside
2. Preheat the oven to 425 F
3. Transfer the sautéed veggies to a baking dish, add remaining ingredients to the baking dish
4. Mix well, add seasoning and place the dish in the oven
5. Bake for 12-15 minutes or until slightly brown
6. When ready remove from the oven and serve

BEAN FRITATTA

Serves: *2*

Prep Time: *10*   Minutes

Cook Time: *20*   Minutes

Total Time: *30*   Minutes

INGREDIENTS

- 1 cup black beans
- 1 tablespoon olive oil
- ½ red onion
- 2 eggs
- ¼ tsp salt
- 2 oz. cheddar cheese
- 1 garlic clove
- ¼ tsp dill

DIRECTIONS

1. In a bowl whisk eggs with salt and cheese
2. In a frying pan heat olive oil and pour egg mixture
3. Add remaining ingredients and mix well
4. Serve when ready

ROASTED SQUASH

Serves:	**3-4**
Prep Time:	**10** Minutes
Cook Time:	**20** Minutes
Total Time:	**30** Minutes

INGREDIENTS

- 2 delicata squashes
- 2 tablespoons olive oil
- 1 tsp curry powder
- 1 tsp salt

DIRECTIONS

1. Preheat the oven to 400 F
2. Cut everything in half lengthwise
3. Toss everything with olive oil and place onto a prepared baking sheet
4. Roast for 18-20 minutes at 400 F or until golden brown
5. When ready remove from the oven and serve

POTATO CHIPS

Serves: *2*
Prep Time: *10*   Minutes

Cook Time: *20*   Minutes

Total Time: *30*   Minutes

INGREDIENTS

- 1 lb. sweet. potatoes
- 2 tablespoons olive oil
- 1 tablespoon smoked paprika
- 1 tablespoon salt

DIRECTIONS

1. Preheat the oven to 425 F
2. In a bowl toss everything with olive oil and seasoning
3. Spread everything onto a prepared baking sheet
4. Bake for 8-10 minutes or until crisp
5. When ready remove from the oven and serve

Serves: **2**

Prep Time: **10**   Minutes

Cook Time: **20**   Minutes

Total Time: **30**   Minutes

INGREDIENTS

- 1 lb. zucchini
- 2 tablespoons olive oil
- 1 tablespoon smoked paprika
- 1 tablespoon salt

DIRECTIONS

1. **Preheat the oven to 425 F**
2. **In a bowl toss everything with olive oil and seasoning**
3. **Spread everything onto a prepared baking sheet**
4. **Bake for 8-10 minutes or until crisp**
5. **When ready remove from the oven and serve**

PIZZA RECIPES

ZUCCHINI PIZZA CRUST

Serves: **4**

Prep Time: **10**   Minutes

Cook Time: **30**   Minutes

Total Time: **40**   Minutes

INGREDIENTS

- 4 zucchinis
- 2 tsp salt
- 2 cups almond flour
- 2 tablespoons coconut flour
- 3 eggs
- 2 ½ cups cheddar cheese
- 1 tsp red pepper flakes
- 1 tsp dried oregano

DIRECTIONS

1. Shred the zucchini, sprinkle with salt and set aside
2. Preheat the oven to 400 F
3. Mix zucchini with remaining ingredients
4. Place the dough over a baking sheet and spread evenly

5. Pop the pizza crust in the oven for 30 minutes or until golden brown

6. When ready, remove and serve

BARBEQUE PIZZA

Serves: **2**

Prep Time: **10** Minutes

Cook Time: **15** Minutes

Total Time: **25** Minutes

INGREDIENTS

- 1 pizza crust
- 1 tsp olive oil
- 1 cup onion
- ¼ cup red pepper strips
- 1 cup cooked chicken
- ¼ cup barbecue sauce
- 1 cup mozzarella cheese

DIRECTIONS

1. In a frying pan add pepper strips, onion and fry until soft
2. Add barbecue sauce, chicken and stir well
3. On a ready-made pizza crust spread onion, pepper mix, chicken and top with mozzarella
4. Bake for 12-15 minutes at 425 F

SHRIMP PIZZA

Serves: **4**

Prep Time: **5**   Minutes

Cook Time: **20**   Minutes

Total Time: **25**   Minutes

INGREDIENTS

- 1 package pizza dough
- 1 tablespoon cornmeal
- 1/3 cup ricotta cheese
- 1 lb. shrimp
- 5 cloves roasted garlic
- 2 ¼ cups mozzarella cheese
- 1 tablespoon basil

DIRECTIONS

1. Stretch pizza dough across a baking pan and bake for 6-8 minutes, sprinkle cornmeal over the pan
2. Mix ricotta cheese, garlic, shrimp together and place over pizza crust
3. Cover pizza with mozzarella and basil
4. Bake for 12-15 minutes at 425 F

CAULIFLOWER CRUST PIZZA

Serves: *4*

Prep Time: *10*   Minutes

Cook Time: *20*   Minutes

Total Time: *30*   Minutes

INGREDIENTS

- 1 lb. ground beef
- 1 egg
- 1 tsp parsley
- 1 tsp dried basil
- ¼ tsp salt
- ½ tsp pepper
- ¼ cup tomato puree
- 1 tsp tomato paste
- ¼ red pepper
- 1 tsp dried basil
- ¼ cup olives
- 5 slices prosciutto
- 4 oz. parmesan
- 1 handful fresh basil

DIRECTIONS

1. Preheat the oven to 430 F
2. In a bowl add salt, mince, egg, basil, pepper, parsley and mix well
3. Roll into a ball and place on a baking tray
4. Bake for 12-15 minutes
5. Mix the tomato paste with tomato puree and spread across the base
6. Top with peppers, prosciutto, parmesan, olives and bake for another 8-10 minutes
7. Remove from the oven, top with basil leaves and serve

THANK YOU FOR READING THIS BOOK!

CPSIA information can be obtained
at www.ICGtesting.com
Printed in the USA
BVHW031357150321
602550BV00001B/305